I0478447

Business Plan Writing

Learn the Secrets of

Writing a Successful Business Plan

Copyright 2017 by David Morales - All rights reserved.

This document is geared towards providing exact and reliable information in regards to the topic and issue covered. The publication is sold with the idea that the publisher is not required to render accounting, officially permitted, or otherwise, qualified services. If advice is necessary, legal or professional, a practiced individual in the profession should be ordered.

- From a Declaration of Principles which was accepted and approved equally by a Committee of the American Bar Association and a Committee of Publishers and Associations.

In no way is it legal to reproduce, duplicate, or transmit any part of this document in either electronic means or in printed format. Recording of this publication is strictly prohibited and any storage of this document is not allowed unless with written permission from the publisher. All rights reserved.

The information provided herein is stated to be truthful and consistent, in that any liability, in terms of inattention or otherwise, by any usage or abuse of any policies, processes, or directions contained within is the solitary and utter responsibility of the recipient reader. Under no circumstances will any legal responsibility or blame be held against the publisher for any reparation, damages, or monetary loss due to the information herein, either directly or indirectly.

Respective authors own all copyrights not held by the publisher.

The information herein is offered for informational purposes solely, and is universal as so. The presentation of the information is without contract or any type of guarantee assurance.

The trademarks that are used are without any consent, and the publication of the trademark is without permission or backing by the trademark owner. All trademarks and brands within this book are for clarifying purposes only and are the owned by the owners themselves, not affiliated with this document.

Table of Contents

Introduction

I would like to thank you for purchasing this book, 'Business Plan Writing - Learn the Secrets of Writing a Successful Business Plan'

A well thought out business plan is quintessential for building enthusiasm for a new idea. It also helps in increasing the likelihood of success. A well-crafted business plan comes in really handy when coming up with a new proposition or even while building a new company. In this book, you will learn all the basics of creating a business plan. You will be able to present your ideas in an unambiguous manner, develop financial plans that are sound, generate risk projections and also anticipate the different rewards that your business can reap.

This book has been designed in such a manner that you will be able to develop a good business plan for generating the necessary enthusiasm you would want for your idea.

A business plan is a blueprint of how you would want to run your business, your expectations, risks, rewards, opportunities and any likely obstacles that you might face. Having a business plan not only gives others an idea of what your business is all about, but it is your guide for going about your daily work.

So, why don't we get started?

Chapter 1: Basics about a Business Plan

To put it simply, a business plan is a guide for your business. It outlines all the goals and different details about how you can go about achieving your objectives. A business plan doesn't have to be a long and a formal document. You are trying to outline your goal, and not write a thesis paper. Having a well thought out and well prepared business plan definitely has some benefits to offer. This also comes in handy when you are looking out for investors or seeking a loan. You can start out with a simple idea and then let it grow. You don't have to include anything that does not serve any purpose for your business.

For instance, describing your management team wouldn't be of any use, unless you are doing so for the benefit of outsiders. You needn't include an exit strategy in your plan unless and until you are writing these down for the sake of your investors. The form will follow function when it comes to business planning. The plan should be about what is going to happen. The final document, a summary memo, and the pitch desk are just certain outputs of this final plan. Writing a business plan is so much simpler these days. Your business plan doesn't have to be a 40 or 50 page document. They are not only easier to write, but are also easier to read and understand. In this chapter, let us take a look at the basic information that you will need to know about business plans.

What is a business plan?

Have you ever penned down a business idea on a napkin or written down the tasks that you need to accomplish on a piece of paper? Well, if you have, then this is one of the most basic components of a business plan. A business plan is a plan of how you want your business to work and the manner in which you can make it a success. A business plan will be much lengthier than the list that you would have written on a napkin. For most types of business, writing down a few bullet points about business strategy, targets to achieve, fiscal estimates and responsibilities is sufficient. A business plan should be printed for certain occasions, like when you need to share some information with outsiders or your team members perhaps. Otherwise, this is something that should be readily accessible to you. You will keep on making additions to the plan; therefore keeping a printed version is redundant.

If you really want to keep a formal business plan on hand, then you will need to include an executive summary, the overview of the company, information about the products or the services offered, your marketing strategy, a list of all the major milestones of your business, information about the management team of the company and the financial plan of your business. The most important of all this would be the review schedule. A real business plan is one that is being reviewed and revised regularly. You will need to keep on updating it so that it stays in synch with the direction in which your business is moving. It is a misconception that only a new business will need a business plan. It is essential for running a business or even for managing finances. Every business will have certain long term as well short term goals, sales and expense budgets. A business plan includes information about all these things.

Who needs a business plan?

If you want to step beyond freelancing work, then you should have a business plan. If you are serious about your business endeavor, planning will be critical to your success.

Startups

The most classic of all the scenarios of business planning is that made for a startup. This plan will help the entrepreneurs to break down their operations into meaningful bits that can be evaluated quite easily. The need for a business plan becomes quite evident when you aren't certain of your financial requirements, and when you might need it, without figuring out your projected sales, costs, expenses and the timing of payments. This is the case for all the startups, irrespective of whether they are trying to convince future investors, banks, friends or even family to fund their venture. In such a case, the business plan would focus on what the company does, how to go about accomplishing the set goals and why the investors should invest in the idea. While making a plan for a startup business, the finances required for getting the venture off the ground should also be mentioned.

Existing businesses

Not only startups, but also even existing businesses, need to have a business plan. This helps in steering the course of the business. It is not just about addressing the various changes in the market, but also for taking advantage of the various opportunities that might come up. A business plan helps in reinforcing the business strategy, for establishing the necessary metrics, measuring goals and performance, tracking results and also for planning and managing the outflow and the inflow of resources. This also helps in making a schedule for revision and review as well. Business plans help in driving the growth of an existing business. It shouldn't be a static document, but should be a dynamic tool that helps in tracking growth and predicting any potential problems before they adversely affect the business.

Selecting the correct plan

A business plan serves multiple purposes. Therefore, there are different forms of business plans. Before you get started with your business plan, you will need to take into consideration the target audience and your goals. There are certain common components that are present in all business plans like sales forecast, marketing strategies and such. Depending on the type of business, the plan will also vary. For instance, if you are planning for a biotech company, then you will need to explain in detail the different government approvals required. If you are writing down a plan for a restaurant, then you should consider things like the location, renovations, the target audience and so on. The language used in both these plans would vary as well. Presentation of these plans could also differ. Plans that are used for internal planning and management might make use of a moral casual language and might not be visually appealing. Whereas, a plan that has been prepared for a venture capitalist would be polished and will focus on the main aspects of the business and the experienced members of the team who would deliver on that promise. Let us take a quick look at the most common types of plans.

A one-page plan is a summary of your business venture that has been described on a single page. This isn't a paper saving gimmick and doesn't mean that you start making use of small font or cram information into one page. This is supposed to be one of the most concise forms of a plan with a to-the-point approach. A plan of this sort helps in serving two uses, the first one being that it is handy for introducing the idea of your business to third parties. An internal business plan is one that is strictly used for internal management and training purposes. It focuses on budgets, forecasts, milestones and different business strategies. An external business plan is also referred to as a regular business plan and it is a formal document that has been designed for providing the much-required information about the business to outsiders. You will learn more about the different business plans in the coming chapters.

Chapter 2: Making Use of Business Plan

Having a business plan gives your business an edge over your competitors. However, it isn't just writing a plan that will grant you success. You will be able to extract the most from a business plan if you start treating it as a tool for management. For doing this, your business plan should be constantly revised and reviewed after taking into consideration the current scenario and any other information that you will have collected. You will learn something new every day. It could be something as simple as what your customers like to something as complex as figuring out the marketing tactics that work. Your business plan should reflect all the things you have observed. It does sound like a lot of work. However, it doesn't necessarily need to be. Let us take a look at some tips that will help you in making the most of your business plan.

Always make use of a one-page business plan for giving a basic outline of your business strategy. Make use of this for reviewing your other strategies as well. For instance, the aspects that you can evaluate are - has your target audience changed? Do you still address the same issues?

An internal plan can be made use of for documenting the processes that are effective. You should share this document with employees as well for giving them a better understanding of your business strategy. Set targets for what you plan on achieving in the next one month. Assign these tasks to different team members, set dates for each target and allocate the resources accordingly. Your sales forecast as well as your expense budget should be static. Compare your planned budgets and even forecasts with the actual performance. This will help you in making the necessary changes. If you really want to make the most of your business plan, then you will need to include a monthly review. This will help in evaluating whether or not your strategy is working, and if so then what can be done to improve the same.

Chapter 3: Various Business Plans

Business plans are referred to by different names like operational plans, internal plans, and even strategic plans. There are lean business plans, one-page business plans, traditional business plans, formal business plans, and so on. You will require these plans at one time or the other during the course of your business. Let us take a look at some of the many types of business plans there are.

Lean business plan

Every business can make use of a lean plan for managing their strategy, tactics, deadlines, business activities and even their cash flow. This is easier to make and more efficient than a regular business plan since it doesn't include any summaries or descriptions. However, it does include certain deadlines, targets and also the allocated budgets for the same. A lean business plan usually includes four essential ingredients.

You will need to set your business strategy and explain the same in simple points. Then you will need to write down the methods by which you can execute this plan. It can include information about your marketing tactics, pricing strategies and so on. Include a list of specifications that you would want to keep a track of like performance measurement and a list of all the assumptions. Keep a track of the essential numbers of the company like its sales forecast, budget and cash flow.

Standard business plan

This is shorter than it used to be and it is one of those documents that would be available online as well as in printed form. This is usually presented when a bank, investor, vendor, ally or even a partner asks for a business plan. Most of the standard business plans include a summary and other sections that cover the information about the business, the products or services it has to offer, target audience, various strategies and the implementation of the same along with the positive results. There is no specific order in which this information needs to be mentioned. A lean plan can be thought of as a first draft of the standard business plan. You can start from there and keep on adding different sections that will help the reader in getting a better idea of your business and operations. There are three important financial projections that you will need to include and these are profit and loss, a balance sheet and the statement of cash flow. All standard business plans will need these three in addition to the sales plan.

The cash flow statement is quintessential when it comes to a business plan. Every business requires cash for meeting its operational requirements. A business will be able to survive without earning profits for a while. However, it will need cash for paying the bills. Profits aren't the only criteria for judging the working of a business, a projected cash flow statement is very important. Some standard plans also include information about personnel spending and other projections. This could include an exit strategy when the times get tough, debt to equity ratio, or any of the other liquidity ratios. This kind of a plan usually starts out with executive summary, key aspects of your plan, and ends with monthly and annual projections for the first and subsequent years respectively. This is usually presented at the beginning of the plan; it makes sense if you leave the executive summary to the very end. This will help in writing an executive summary that is well thought out and includes all the necessary information.

Business plan for startups

Every startup needs a business plan for breaking down the steps and different requirements with calculated guesses for keeping a track of important lists and numbers. The business plan of a startup is also referred to as startup plan. It is a general misconception that business plans are only devised for startups. That's definitely not the case; business planning is a part of management. Usually, a lean business plan is used as a startup plan and it includes projections about costs, strategies and targets. The startup costs consist of such expenses that have been incurred before the business has been launched. A lean plan with certain additional information tends to be perfectly fine for most business startups. However, when a startup starts requiring additional funding, then the startup will need to be a standard business plan. You can also make use of this plan for discussing your options with any of the potential partners as well as associates. This is a no-frills plan and helps in deciding whether or not an idea is worth going ahead with. You can always make any additional changes to your business plan as your business grows. When a startup plan is given to an outsider, it will be helpful if you can add an executive summary, company overview and details of the management team, market description, a marketing plan and your product plan as well. You needn't have the exact estimates, even a preliminary analysis would do.

One-page business plan

A one-page plan is exactly what the name suggests. This is a one-page summary and it includes the highlights of your business. It also helps in summarizing the target market, the business offering, any targets that were achieved and even a sales forecast. This form of a plan comes in really handy when you are explaining about your business to banks, prospective investors, vendors and even employees. This is also referred to as a business pitch.

Internal Plan

Internal plans are quite similar to lean plans. These help in reflecting the needs of the various members of the company or business. These plans are specific to the needs and requirements of all those who are a part of the company; those who are directly involved in the workings of the business. These plans are usually concise and short. These plans are solely designed for the internal management of the business.

Feasibility plan

A few experts usually make use of this phrase as a synonym for a startup plan. Others tend to use it for referring to certain steps that are taken for validating a technology, product or a marketplace. For instance, this type of a plan used for the introduction of a new type of brick oven may have the demo version created in a lab, a prototype for testing whether or not it works, and a working product. It would include getting a few early users and then making them validate the idea as to whether or not people might want to spend any money on the product. In some cases it also means making the product available on a website, making it available in advance to check whether or not people would commit to it. These plans usually don't include the wide range of topics that are usually included in a regular or a lean business plan. This, instead, focuses on whether or not a product idea is feasible and whether it would work in the market.

Annual plan

These plans are akin to lean plans too. Similar to a lean plan, even these include the specific implementation targets; any project deadlines that need to be met and the responsibilities of various members of the management. These plans are made use of for making sure that you are staying on track and that the goals that you have set for a business are being met. Planning based on the goals set will allow you to decide your priorities, focus on the results and keep a track of your progress. These plans would cover information about all the inner workings of the business. It will provide outlines for certain specifications regarding what needs to be done and who should do it.

Expansion plan

Either these plans could be lean plans or even standard business plans. However, these are focused on a specific area of the business. For instance, a plan that has been designed with the intention of creating a new product is referred to as a growth plan. These plans can be both internal and external depending upon whether or not these plans are being linked for the application of a loan or an investment. An expansion plan that requires a new investment from outside would need to include certain descriptions about the business, the market, management team, some information about the product and so on. Even a loan application would require all these details. An internal growth plan, on the other hand, wouldn't need all these steps.

Strategic plan

A strategic plan is another phrase that people tend to make use of

17

according to different contexts. A strategic plan is an internal plan, but without all the different specifications and financial projections. It generally includes more details about the strategy and the different tactics that are to be used than a lean plan would do. It includes more description and explanations. However, what good would a strategy do without it being executed? A good strategic plan should take the implementation aspect into consideration as well. This means resources and time should also be taken into account.

As you start developing the strategy for your business and also decide on the way in which you can implement it, you should also examine the strengths and weaknesses of the business. What are the positives of your business? What does your company do better than others? As your business starts to grow, you should start playing to your strengths. Strategy is simply the matter of selecting the correct opportunities. Resources need to be funneled in a strategic manner to the areas that will provide you the most benefits out of each particular area or field. For effectively executing the strategies, it is incredibly important that you assign certain responsibilities and then stick to a schedule that you should follow. The implementation of these tactics will help you in moving ahead in the right direction for achieving the goals set. This is the very purpose for which a business plan is written.

Writing a business plan

Writing a business plan is really easy. Your business plan should be short and precise. There is no reason for it to be a lengthy document. It is supposed to provide the reader with an idea of what your business is all about. The plan should be written while keeping in mind the kind of audience who would read it. Making use of complicated jargon will get you nowhere. Don't get intimidated and simply include all the information that has been mentioned in the foregoing chapters.

Chapter 4: Initial Assessment

Assessment is an important aspect in any business plans to identify the basics. Therefore, it is always good to start a business plan with an assessment

Let it be an operating model that is ongoing. It is important to look into the basics and loot at the numbers and ask questions to see if they make sense? This is to understand if it is worth starting.

Objectives

Milestones are always important for any business plan to succeed, right market share, the sales strategy and margin numbers. It is extremely important to achieve these for which it is mandatory to plan.

These milestones need to be solid, futuristic and realistic. These should be able to be tracked and analyzed, like market share, growth, profit percentage and revenue. Superlatives like state of the art and exponential growth would not be measurable and are very generic.

Milestones can be defined by using superlatives like extraordinary, maximize customer experience, but are not result oriented as they cannot be measured. Key performance indicators such as 25% growth, sales more than $5 million, year on year growth of 5% would be realistic and measurable.

Milestones that are not measurable are less critical to be planned. It is very important to plan them. To measure goals that cannot be number driven, one needs to create an alternative to achieve the same, such as surveys to measure awareness.

Mission Statement

Before setting up any company, it is important to have a business plan based on the milestones defined and strategies that drive the company.

What business you are in

Passion is always the driving factor for setting up a business of your own. It is very important to understand the business you are in. The options are always wide open and narrowing down your ideas would not be the greatest way to handle planning. Railroads are one of the best examples. It lost a chance to expand, as they had not identified themselves. The agenda of transporting goods and people were the key businesses it was into. They had not realized the potential of the company. When alternative transport systems increased like trucks, buses were available and highways grew, the railroads couldn't cope with it and were left behind. It is always important to have a holistic approach in order to understand the goal.

Customer satisfaction:

Many companies who believe in customer satisfaction as a goal look to their mission statement. Customer centric programs would depend a lot on the concept of spreading an idea and the importance of that idea. This should easily be gleaned from a mission statement.

Workplace philosophy

Mission statements need not be required to be external as they can be useful internally. The internal goals such as maintaining a healthy, creative environment and a rich diversity can be underlined in the mission statement. The mission statement should define and the company should stick by these fundamentals.

Value-based marketing

Value based marketing would help people to understand the business better. It starts with a value proposition, benefits that the business offers and the price level.

Keys to success

Setting priorities would depend on the key success areas and focusing on these is of utmost importance. Any business depends on four or five critical factors. Focus is the key parameter and a right approach, methodology and framework helps in focus. If more priorities are on the list, the chance of implementation is much less. These key factors and focus around them are the success mantras for any business to work.

Break-even analysis

Estimating the time that it would take for your business to start making profits is very important. A simple break-even analysis would help you in understanding your fixed costs, variable costs and revenue. For any break-even analysis, these are the parameters defined:

Average Sales price per unit: It is the price of the product per unit. It would be calculated based on discounts and offers. For businesses that are not product driven, the costs are entered as a percentage of a dollar.

Average Per Unit Cost: The cost of per unit value of the product. For manufacturing businesses, they can project unit costs from a sales forecast table.

Monthly Fixed: These are the costs that are recurring and would continue even if you go bankrupt. Running costs would give you a great insight on the financial realities and these include payroll costs and normal expenditure.

The profit increases as the sales increase and when break-even is reached, the profit line will reach the line where it was breakeven or zero.

Market analysis

Understanding the market and to analyze if there was a sufficient scope for running your business. A major research is not really required for the initial analysis. However, as it progresses the research should increase. In the initial stages, it is important for one to understand the target customers and potential business. Realistically it is very important to calculate break-even point post this phase, as you have to look into the customer base that you might have to break even. Then one needs to develop an analysis table for markets, to segregate each segment and the customers within that segment. These customers are divided according to the need, for example: the supply, areas, preferences etc. depending on the nature of business. Total customers and the annual growth rate have to be captured in the table.

Pause for reflection

At this phase, it is important to hold back and check the status of the planning performed. Business has been defined, the financial break-even point has been established and also we have an idea of the potential market share for the business. Further, one needs to have a third party view of the how the business might look from an outside perspective? Can we reach the break-even that was anticipated? Is it big enough to proceed and are your targets realistic? This is an important check for all startups. Many people dream of having the best business plan. However, these dreams turn into a nightmare. If there is a potential doubt in the approach, then it is better to revisit the plan or idea or give up and try for a better solution.

Chapter 5: What to Include in a Business Plan

Now that you are familiar with the rules of writing a business plan, we can get started with building your business plan. The following things should be included in your business plan.

Executive summary

Technically, this is the first part of your business plan. However, it is advisable if you write this in the very end. It is easier to write a better summary about your business once you are fully aware of all the details needed. The executive summary can be thought of as the introduction to your company and what it does, and lays down information about what you are looking for from the readers. The executive summary will cover the important points that are included in your detailed plan. Investors usually tend to ask for only the executive summary for the evaluation of businesses. The executive summary indeed is a critical component of your plan and it needs to concise and crystal clear. You should be able to include information about all the highlights of your business without getting into too many details. It shouldn't be more than one or two pages. Anything more than this and the investor would lose interest. Let us take a look at some of the components that need to be included in the business plan.

You should include a one-sentence business overview, right under the name of your business. This should portray the essence of your business. It can even be a tagline. However, it should effectively describe the objective of your business. Address the problem that your business is solving and the need that it is fulfilling in the market. Once you have described the problem, write about the product or services that you are offering for solving this problem. Then you will need to identify your target customers. If you happen to be a shoe company, then you definitely won't be targeting everyone, and would be catering only to a certain demographic or segment of the market such as sports, etc.

Once you have identified the target market, you will need to check how your competitors are going about doing business. You will need to provide an overview of your team, and state why they are best suited for taking forward your ideas to the world. Investors tend to concentrate more on the team; therefore don't forget to include this. Provide a financial summary by including your sales projections, expenses and also your profitability. If you want to raise money for your business or you are looking forward to expanding, then you should also make note of your funding requirements. Include a short and precise statement to show how much funds you will require. Lastly, you will also need to include any milestones or achievements that you have unlocked. This will show your willingness to improve and also provide your investors or customers with data that shows that your product or service is working. If you are writing a business plan for internal management, then you can afford to skip the executive summary.

Company Overview

This will perhaps be the shortest bit of your business plan. If you are making an internal plan, then you can skip this one as well. This section should include the following details when made for external purposes:

It should include **your mission statement**. You needn't have to spend a lot of time or money on your mission statement. It shouldn't be a long and generic statement. It could be just one or two sentences long and it should reflect your overall proposition. The overview of your company should also include a summary of the existing legal structure. Whether your business is a sole proprietorship, a partnership, a corporation, or even an LLC? Potential investors would like to know **the legal structure and the ownership of the business** before making an investment. If you are writing a business plan for an existing company, then you should include a **brief history of the company**, its operations, and achievements. This section should be short and crisp. It helps in giving context to the rest of the plan. Don't forget to include a **description of your existing location** and other facilities owned by the business.

Products and Services

This is the real deal. This section will help you in describing in great detail the problem that you are addressing, the solution and the manner in which your product or service will help in providing you with an edge over your competitors. Much of this will already be included in the executive summary. However, this is an important section and helps in answering questions that haven't already been covered in the executive summary.

Problem and the solution

You should start this section by describing the problem that the target audience is facing and the manner in which you can solve it. What are their main grievances and how are they resolving it? Maybe the solutions that are available are too expensive, or they

27

are just cumbersome. If you have managed to identify the problem that is troubling your potential customers, then you have a viable business idea. Defining not just the problem but also the manner in which you are solving it is one of the most important elements of a business plan. This can make or break your business. For making sure that you are in fact solving an actual problem, a step in the process of business planning is to move away from your desk and talk to your target audience. Confirm whether or not the problem that you think they have is actually a problem. Once you know what the problem is, will your solution be of any help? After describing the problem, you will need to describe the solution in detail. What is it and how can your company help to solve it? For certain products and services, you will need to describe the various uses they possess as well.

Competition

Once you have described the problem and the solution for the same, it is time to describe your competition. Who else in the market is providing the same services and what are your advantages over those of your competition? Most business plans tend to make use of a competitor matrix for listing out competitors and to see how their ideas compare with your ideas. It is very easy to build a competitor matrix. You will need to list down the names of your competitors on the left side and then keep on adding columns for each of the features. You can make use of checkmarks for listing out the features that your competitors offer. The one thing that you should highlight in this section is the advantage that your business offers over the competitors. Stating that they haven't got any competition is one of the most common mistakes that an entrepreneur could make while drafting a business plan.

All businesses will have competition. It doesn't always have to be direct competition; it could be indirect competition as well. For instance, when Henry Ford had first started marketing cars there wasn't much direct completion from other manufacturers. However, he was competing with different forms of transport like carriages, trains and so on. Some companies should also provide the information that has been mentioned below.

If your business is acquiring products from different vendors, then it is important to mention details about where the products came from, the manner in which you got them delivered, and the how they would reach the ultimate consumers. If your products are being sourced from manufacturers settled overseas, then potential investors would be interested in knowing about any progress that you have made. If you are a technology based company, then you will need to describe the kind of technology you are dealing in and how this is different from that which is otherwise available on the market. You needn't start mentioning about any "trade secrets" here. Just add some information that will help in making your product seem more competitive.

If your business owns any intellectual property, then the information intimating the same should be mentioned here. If you have any patents, or any patent applications, then this is the place to mention it. Technology licensing should be mentioned as well. It would be good if you could include some information about any future products or services that you might offer in the future.

Target Market

Now that you have given a detailed description of all the products and services that you are offering, it is time to direct your attention towards the target audience, your target market. Depending on the kind of business that you are starting and also the kind of plan that you are writing, you might not have to explain things in great detail here. Regardless of anything, you will need to have a rough idea of who your target audience is. If research shows that there aren't many potential customers for your product or service, then think of this as a warning sign. If you want to conduct market analysis, this is the area in which you will need to do some research - firstly, for identifying the market segments that you can target and then for determining the size of these segments. A market segment comprises of a group of people or even other business to whom you could cater. Be wary and don't fall into the trap of trying to define your market segment as "everyone." A good business plan should help you in identifying the different market segments that you can target, and provide you with the necessary data for indicating the growth rate of each of these segments.

For identifying the different market segments, there are certain methods that are usually used. These are TAM, SOM and SAM, TAM, which stand for Total Available Market, and it refers to the market segment or those whom you are targeting. SAM stands for Segmented Addressable Market and it stands for that portion of TAM who you will be targeting. SOM means Share of the Market and this is a subset of SAM; the realistic portion of SAM that you will be able to target. Once you have managed to identify the essential market segments, then you can get started with discussing the trends that exist in these markets. Is it growing or shrinking, the evolving needs and preferences, or any other changes?

Once you have managed to identify your market segments, then you will need to define the "ideal" customer in each of these segments. Ideal customers can be thought of as a representation of your target market and is referred to as the buyer persona. The characteristics that you should take into consideration while defining the buyer persona should be names, gender, age, likes, dislikes and so on. This might just seem like a lot of unnecessary work, but it does come in really handy when you have these details.

Key customers

Now it is time to start discussing key customers. This section is necessary for those businesses that tend to have few customers, like enterprise companies. If you are selling to other businesses, then there are only a few customers who would be considered to be essential for the success of your business. There might be a few customers who can also be thought of as the trendsetters and these few have got the power to influence the preferences of everyone else in the market.

Marketing and Sales plan

This section of the business plan contains details on how you will be able to reach your target audience, your sales plan for the target market, pricing structure and the types of activities that you will need to undertake for achieving success in your business. Before you get started with writing a marketing plan, you will need to have a well-defined target market and also have your buyer persona sketched out and defined. Without truly understanding for whose sake you are marketing, you will not be able to have a worthy marketing plan.

Positioning

The initial part of your marketing plan will be about your market positioning and the type of products or services that are on offer. Positioning is all about the manner in which you would want your business to be presented to the customers. Will yours be a low-price, luxury, or a budget brand in the market? Or do you offer something that is different from the ones that your competitors have on offer? Before you can start writing your positioning statement, you will need to take some time and evaluate the current market conditions.

Answer the following questions and you will be able to get a feel of the market conditions. What are the features or the different benefits that you offer and how does it differ from the ones offered by your competitors? What are the primary needs of your customers? The way your competitors are positioned when compared to you? How do you plan on standing apart in the crowd? To put it simply, why should the customer choose you and not someone else? Once you have answered all these questions, then you can start working on your positioning strategy and include it in your business plan. Your positioning statement doesn't have to be really long or even very elaborate. You just need to explain how your company would compare with its competitors in the market.

Pricing

Once you are aware of your positioning strategy, the next aspect that you will need to focus on would be the price. Your positioning strategy will have a major impact on your pricing strategy as well. You can send a strong message to not just the customers but also your competitors through your pricing strategy. If you have got a premium product to offer and it has a premium price tag, then this will convey the same effectively to the consumers. Deciding on a price is not a simple task. There are certain rules that you should take into consideration while doing so. Your pricing strategy should be capable of covering your costs. There are a few exceptions to this.

To put it simply, the price that you are charging your customers should be higher than the cost that you have incurred. The initial price that you might have set wouldn't help you earn a profit immediately. You might have to start at a level that is less than the cost incurred. However, with the lapse of time you can start increasing the price. Your prices will need to keep in synch with the demands of the consumers and their expectations as well. If your product is priced too low, people might tend to undervalue it and if it is set too high, they might think of it as being extravagant.

Your pricing strategy will be based on several different factors. Take a look at your costs and then you can mark up your offering from there. This is referred to as "cost plus pricing." This method of pricing is quite useful for manufacturer while they are covering their initial costs of doing business. The other method would be to take a look at the present market scenario, your competitors, and base your price on what the market expects. Your price range could be high end or low end, and this will help you in deciding your positioning. There is another pricing method that can be made use of as well. This is referred to as "value-pricing." In this method, the price is determined based on the value that you are expecting to provide to your customer.

Promotion

Since pricing and positioning have been taken care of, now we can move on to the promotion strategy. A promotion plan essentially describes the manner in which you would want to communicate with your prospective customers. The following areas should be included in your promotional plan. The first one is packaging. If you have decided to sell a product, then the packaging of that product is of vital importance. Is your packaging in synch with your positioning strategy? Your key value proposition needs to be communicated via your packaging. How does it fare in comparison with your competition? Having images of your packaging in your business plan would be a good idea. Your advertising plan should be included in your business plan. Will you opt for online advertising? Or any other form of traditional media? You need to include a component for measuring the success of your advertising plan within your advertising plan. Public relations are a key aspect of your promotional strategy. You can reach out to a wider customer base by making use of media.

Getting good reviews for your products or services will also help in creating a positive reaction for the same in the market. Content marketing is considered to be a good promotional strategy. Business plans are all about content marketing. When you start publishing useful information, tips, or even advice, your target audience will start to get to know about your business and the kind of expertise that you offer. Usually such information is provided free of cost. Content marketing is also about engaging your prospective customers on topics that might interest them. Social media is the best platform for promoting anything these days. Having a strong presence on social media will definitely come in handy. You needn't have to be on every single social media network. However, it would be really helpful to be on the ones that most of your customers tend to access. For product companies, a distribution plan is extremely important aspect of a business plan. A service providing company can usually do away with this step.

Distribution is the manner in which you will be able to get your product or service to your prospective customers. Every industry would have a different channel for distribution. The best manner in which you can create a distribution plan is by interviewing others who are a part of the same industry as you and understand their distribution model. A few commonly used distribution models are direct distribution, retail distribution, manufacturer's representatives, and OEM. In direct distribution, as the name suggests, the products are directly sold to the consumers and this is the most profitable option that is available. If you don't like the hassle of having to deal with multiple individual suppliers, then retail distribution is the best option that is available for you. You needn't have to select only one channel of distribution either. Most of the companies and businesses these days tend to make use of a combination of more than one channel of distribution. You might have to start working with another company or business as a partnership for your marketing plan. This partnership might provide you the necessary access to your target market and it would allow your partner to offer something new to their customers as well. If you have an already existing partnership, then you should disclose the same in the business plan as well. Without implementation, a plan is just a document.

The milestones and the metrics part of your business might not be really lengthy, it is important that you take some time out for looking ahead and schedule the next step that your business needs to take. Investors will definitely want to know what is going on and the manner in which you will be able to make your targets into a reality. There needs to be a realistic schedule that can be implemented. You can start out by quickly reviewing all the milestones. Milestones can be thought of as goals or major targets.

For instance, if you were in the business of the production of a medical device, then you milestone probably would be associated with the phase of clinical testing or even approvals from the government.

Milestones are prospective in nature. However, you should also stop for a moment and take into consideration all your major accomplishments; the things that you have already achieved and this is referred to as traction. This is the evidence that your business is growing and it has more potential in store. Your business plan should also include a mention of certain key metrics that you will need to keep a watchful eye on if you want to be able to get your business started. Metrics are the numbers that you will need to monitor constantly for judging the performance of your business. They are the units through which you can judge whether or not your business is performing the way it is supposed to.

For instance, in an establishment like a restaurant, special attention would need to be given to the average number of table turns that they might have on every night and the ration of drink to food sales. Every business will have different key metrics that it will need to monitor their growth. Being aware of your assumptions at the beginning of the business will be the difference between success and failure of your business. Finally, the business plan should also have a detailed description of all the major assumptions that are considered to be important for your business. Thinking about risks is also a manner in which you can start thinking about key assumptions. What risks are worth taking? For instance, if there is no proven demand for a particular product, then you are making an assumption that the target market segment would indeed want the product that you are building? When you have recognized your assumptions, then you can start working towards proving them correct. The less your assumptions are, the better your business will be.

Management Team

There is an old belief that investors invest in people and not in ideas. Some investors might want to invest in a mediocre idea backed by a great team, rather than invest in a brilliant idea with a substandard team. This simply means that when it comes to success in a business, it is all about execution. Ideas are of some value only after they have been implemented and executed in the manner that they were supposed to be. The key to running a successful business is all about execution. If you are able to accomplish all that you have planned for, there is no looking back. If you have got the right team in place, execution becomes really easy.

The section describing the management team of your business will enable you to put forth the best argument that you have got a really capable team in place who can execute the idea in the manner it is supposed to be executed. It also shows that you have given considerable thought to what the important roles as well as responsibilities are for your business. This section of the business plan should include brief descriptions or bios of all the members of the team, their experience, and any other achievements. It is incredibly important that you make a case for why the team that you have on hand is capable of turning the idea into reality.

Do they possess the experience and/or the skill required? A common mistake that budding entrepreneurs make is that they end up giving everyone a C-level title (CEO, CFO, COO, CMO, and so on). This might boost their egos. However, this doesn't do any good for the business. As the company starts to grow, you will start requiring varied experience and knowledge. It is wiser if you provide a provision for the future growth of these titles instead of starting right from the top. There should always be some room for growth. If not, stagnation can contaminate the business.

You needn't necessarily have a complete management team in place for completing your business plan. If there are any gaps in the team, it is okay. In fact, the investors would most likely think that the fact that you know you is missing certain important people as a sign of maturity and knowledge. These are the key components for garnering success. If you know that there are certain gaps in your management team, then you should perhaps identify those gaps and fill them with suitable candidates. You should also include an organizational chart in the business plan. This is not an important component and you can include it in the appendix of the plan. An organization chart is often asked for when it comes to funding. It will also help you in thinking about the key roles that you will need to fill in the future as well.

Financial Plan

Now we are moving on to another extremely important section of the business plan and this is the financial plan. This is considered to be quite daunting by a lot of entrepreneurs. However, it definitely doesn't have to be as intimidating as you might think it can be. Business financials aren't as complicated as people think they are. You don't need to have a degree in business studies for drawing up a financial plan. If you feel that you need some more help for getting things right, then you can always make use of the various online tools for the same. A basic financial plan would have financial projections for a whole year on a monthly basis, and then the annual projections for the next three or five years. The three-year projections will do, however some investors prefer to have five-year projections for better use as well. The following are the details regarding what needs to be included within a financial statement in your business plan.

You will need to have a sales forecast. A sales forecast is the projection of the sales that you are expecting to transact over the period of few years. A sales forecast can be essentially broken down into several parts for each of the key product or service that is on offer. You needn't have to explain all this in great detail. Focus on the major groups. If you own a restaurant, then the sales forecast can be segmented into groups like lunch, dinner and drinks.

The sales forecast should also include a row for each of the sales to mention about something that is referred to as Cost of Goods Sold or COGS. This will help in getting a bird's eye view of the costs and expenses incurred for making your product. You should include only such costs that are directly related to the making of the product and not regular expenses like salaries, rent, electricity, water bills and so on. For a restaurant, the COGS would be the cost of the ingredients procured. For a product company it would be the costs incurred for collecting the necessary raw materials.

The personnel plan will help in writing down the details regarding the payments being made to all the personnel in the business. For a small business, you might have to list out every position that is available and the amount that is being paid to them at the end of each month. For a bigger company, the personnel plan is usually broken down into smaller and more manageable groups like finance, marketing and sales. The personnel plan also includes something that is referred to as an employee burden. This is the cost that the business has to incur, above and beyond the salary that is paid to an employee. It typically includes taxes on payroll, insurance and other necessary costs that are incurred for retaining the employee.

The profit and loss or the P&L statement is also referred to as the Income Statement and this is where all the numbers are brought together. This is where you will know whether or not your business is making a profit or a loss. The costs incurred along with the income earned will help you in assessing the financial health of your business. All the data that is present in the P&L is from the sales forecast, the personnel plan, and other ongoing and recurring expenses necessary for the functioning of the business. A P&L sheet would include information about the revenue incurred from sales. This is where you will need the figures from your sales forecast. The COGS are also collected from the sales forecast: the gross profit and the net profit. Any expenses that are incurred in the form of salaries, employee expenditure, taxes, depreciation, maintenance expenses, regularly incurred expenses like monthly bills. Everything and anything that would have a direct impact on the profits of the business will be included here.

The cash flow statement and the profit and loss statement are usually thought of to be the same thing. This is however not true. The P&L keeps a track of your profits and losses whereas the cash flow statement is just concerned with keeping track of all the cash in the business. You can easily understand the difference between these two by simply understanding the difference between cash and profits earned. If you make a sale and receive the payment on a later on date, you wouldn't include this is your cash flow statement.

However, this sale will be immediately reflected in your P&L statement as an income. The cash flow statement will help you keep a track of the amount of cash that the business has in hand at any given point of time. The most important of all the financial statements is the balance sheet. The balance sheet is the final financial statement. It helps in judging the overall health of the business. The assets and liabilities of the companies are included in here. You will be able to determine the net worth of your business by subtracting the liabilities from the assets owned.

One last thing that you should include in your financial plan would be the exit strategy. An exit strategy is required if ever you would want to sell your business. If you have got any investors, then they will need to know your exit strategy in case of winding up, especially since they have got a stake in the business. They would definitely want to know the returns that they can expect. You don't have to explain all this in great detail. A brief overview would do.

Appendix

Your business plan will also need an appendix. This isn't a compulsory inclusion. However, having one will definitely come in handy when you have got to include charts, tables, definitions, legal notes and any other form of critical information. Information that was probably too long or tedious to understand if placed elsewhere in the plan can be included here. If you have a patent, a copyright, any product design, or other illustrations of the same, then you can include   all   this   in   the   appendix.

Business Plan Template

1.0 Executive Summary

1.1 Problem Statement
1.2 Approach and Methodology
1.3 Understanding the Market
1.4 Structured Competition
1.5 Key Numbers

2.0 Delivery

2.1 Analytical Skills
2.2 Solution offerings
2.3 Mapping of problems to solutions
2.4 Way Forward

3.0 Analysis of Market

3.1 Market Distribution/ Segmentation
3.2 Untapped Market Segmentation
3.2.1 Demand & Supply
3.2.2 Trends
3.2.3 Growth
3.3 Customer Base
3.4 Predictive Analysis of the Markets
3.5 Competition
3.5.1 Alternatives
3.5.2 Key Benefits

4.0 Strategy and Implementation Summary

4.1 Plan for Marketing
4.2 Sales Plan

Conclusion

I would like to thank you once again for purchasing this book.

By now, you will have understood how important a business plan is for your business venture. It is important that you are able to create an effective business strategy if you want to succeed. In this book, you have learnt about what should and shouldn't be included in a business plan. You have also learned what a business plan does and the manner in which you should go about creating one. Developing a business plan doesn't have to be as intimidating as you thought it was. Being able to project your idea onto paper comes in quite handy for a new business. Even existing businesses should have a good business plan.

I believe this book shared you all the necessary information you needed to know for business plans and apply it to your business in order to writing a successful business plan.

The next step is to implement what you have learnt.

Finally, if you enjoyed this book and received value out of it then I'd like to ask you for a favor. Would you be kind enough to leave a review for this book on Amazon? It'd be greatly appreciated!

Leaving review only takes a few seconds and it will enable me to continue to produce high quality, enriching content to serve people like you.

www.ingramcontent.com/pod-product-compliance
Lightning Source LLC
Chambersburg PA
CBHW061450180526
45170CB00004B/1639